SERHAN SARI

Python for Beginners: A Step-by-Step Introduction to Programming with Python

Building a Strong Foundation in Python Programming for Absolute Beginners

This book is dedicated to spirited learners and budding programmers who dare to embark on a journey of discovery through code.

To every individual who dares to dream, to create, and to challenge the boundaries of what's possible, this book is dedicated to you. May your passion for learning and your curiosity about the world of programming continue to fuel your ambitions and drive you toward endless possibilities.

With admiration and encouragement,
Serhan Sarı

"Most good programmers do programming not because they expect to get
paid or get adulation by the public, but
because it is fun to program."

Linus Torvalds

Contents

Preface

Welcome to the wonderful world of programming! "Python for Beginners: A Step-by-Step Introduction to Programming with Python" is more than simply a book; it's a handbook built for inquiring minds, aspiring programmers, and those ready to embrace the art and science of coding.

This book serves as a gateway for absolute beginners, devoid of any prior coding knowledge. Its mission is to unveil the mysteries of Python—a beautiful, versatile, and widely appreciated programming language. Python's simplicity and readability make it a great partner on your trip into the domain of coding.

Within these pages, you'll discover an organized and approachable approach aimed at exposing you to the essential concepts of programming. Whether you're a student exploring new frontiers, a professional trying to develop your skill set, or an enthusiast intrigued by the magic of coding, this book has been precisely customized to be your companion in your earliest steps into the intriguing universe of Python.

Each chapter is intentionally designed, delivering a hands-on experience reinforced by clear explanations and practical examples. The goal is not merely to teach Python but to empower you with the tools and knowledge to solve issues, think logically, and create real-world applications.

The trip you're about to embark on will be an exhilarating one, filled with obstacles, victories, and a profound sense of accomplishment. Remember, the journey to understanding programming is not about reaching a destination; it's a constant, ever-evolving expedition.

At the core of this book is not just technical knowledge but also the essence of endurance and the joy of creation. Your acquired skills in Python will serve as the basis upon which you can build your coding dreams.

So, with enthusiasm and resolve, dive into the pages ahead. Allow your imagination to soar, your reasoning to sharpen, and your creativity to blossom. Accept the difficulties, savor the "aha" experiences, and above all, have fun with the process.

Thank you for visiting "Python for Beginners: A Step-by-Step Introduction to Programming with Python." Together, let's embark on this thrilling voyage.

Acknowledgement

The path to creating "Python for Beginners: A Step-by-Step Introduction to Programming with Python" was made possible by the commitment and encouragement of many amazing people.

Above all, we would like to express our sincere gratitude to all of the readers—beginners as well as aspiring programmers—who made this book their traveling companion while learning to code. Throughout this project, we have been guided by your excitement and desire to learn.

We would like to express our sincere gratitude to the Python community for all of its support, contributions, and abundance of resources, which have greatly enhanced and inspired this book. Your enthusiasm for imparting knowledge has served as a never-ending source of motivation.

We would especially like to thank our team of editors, developers, and contributors who devoted their knowledge, skills, and time to making this book thorough and high-quality. This project is a reality because of your dedication to making programming interesting and approachable for novices.

We are indebted to the trailblazers and instructors whose pioneering work in Python has opened doors for innumerable students. Your insight and direction have greatly influenced the content of this book.

Finally, I would like to express my gratitude to all of my friends, family, and loved ones for their patience, understanding, and belief in the value of education and knowledge sharing along this journey. You have all been an invaluable source of support and encouragement.

This book is a monument to the programming community's collaborative spirit and the group's joint endeavor to enable everyone to learn to code. We appreciate the contributions made by all individuals, regardless of size, towards making "Python for Beginners" a reality.

Learn the Basics

Hello World!

The most basic way to display the string "Hello, World!" is to use the print() function.

The print() function takes a string or other data type as an argument and prints it to the console. Here's an example:

```
print("Hello, World!")
```

When you run this code, it will output the string "Hello, World!" to the console.

Another way to display "Hello, World!" in python is to use the built-in input() function. It allows the user to enter a string and assign it to a variable.

```python
x = input("Hello, World!")
```

This will prompt the user to enter a string and assign it to the variable x.

You can also use the input() function without any parameter, which will prompt the user to input a string and return it as the result of the function call.

```python
x = input()
print("Hello, World!")
```

This way, the user will input the data, and the print function will display "Hello, World!".

You can also use f-strings (Python 3.6+), which is a more efficient and readable way to include a variable inside a string.

```python
name = "world"
print(f"Hello, {name}!")
```

This will return Hello, world!

Indentation:
   Python uses indentation for blocks instead of curly braces. Both tabs and spaces are supported, but the standard indentation requires standard Python code to use four spaces.

For example:
```
x = 1
if x == 1:
# indented four spaces print("x is 1.")
```

Variables and Types

A variable is a named location in memory where a value can be stored. Variables are used to store data and are used in almost every programming language. To create a variable in Python, you need to use an assignment operator (=) and a variable name. The variable name can be any combination of letters, numbers, and underscores, but it cannot begin with a number.

For example:

```
x = 5
y = "hello"
z = [1, 2, 3]
```

Python has several built-in data types, including:

- Numbers: int (integer), float (floating point number), and complex (complex number)
- Strings: used to represent text
- Lists: used to store a collection of items
- Tuples: similar to lists but are immutable
- Dictionaries: used to store key-value pairs

- Boolean: used to represent true or false values
- None: used to represent the absence of a value

You can check the type of any variable by using the type() function.

```
x = 5
print(type(x)) # Output: <class 'int'>
y = "hello"
print(type(y)) # Output: <class 'str'>
z = [1, 2, 3]
print(type(z)) # Output: <class 'list'>
```

Python is a dynamically typed language, which means that the type of a variable is determined at runtime, not at the time of declaring it.

Lists

A list is a collection of items that can be of any data type (strings, numbers, etc.). Lists are enclosed in square brackets ([]), and the items are separated by commas. Here is an example of a list:

```
fruits = ["apple", "banana", "orange"]
```

You can access the elements of a list by using their index, which starts at 0. Here's an example:

```
fruits = ["apple", "banana", "orange"]
print(fruits[0]) # Output: "apple"
print(fruits[1]) # Output: "banana"
```

You can also use negative indexing, which starts counting from the end of the list.

```
fruits = ["apple", "banana", "orange"]
print(fruits[-1]) # Output: "orange"
```

Python lists have many built-in methods that can be used to perform various operations on them. Some common list methods include the following:

- append(item): adds an item to the end of the list
- extend(iterable): adds all the items in an iterable (e.g. a list) to the end of the list
- insert(index, item): inserts an item at a specific index in the list
- remove(item): removes the first occurrence of an item from the list
- pop(index): removes and returns the item at a specific index in the list
- index(item): returns the index of the first occurrence of an item in the list
- count(item): returns the number of occurrences of an item

in the list
- sort(): sorts the items in the list in ascending order
- reverse(): reverses the order of the items in the list
- clear(): removes all items from the list

Here's an example of using some of these methods:

```python
fruits = ["apple", "banana", "orange"]
fruits.append("mango")
print(fruits) # Output: ["apple", "banana", "orange", "mango"]
fruits.insert(1, "kiwi")
print(fruits) # Output: ["apple", "kiwi", "banana", "orange", "mango"]
fruits.remove("banana")
print(fruits) # Output: ["apple", "kiwi", "orange", "mango"]
fruits.pop(2)
print(fruits) # Output: ["apple", "kiwi", "mango"]
fruits.sort()
print(fruits) # Output: ["apple", "kiwi", "mango"]
fruits.reverse()
print(fruits) # Output: ["mango", "kiwi", "apple"]
```

You can also use slicing to access a subset of a list. The syntax is list[start:end:step]. start is the starting index of the slice, end is the ending index of the slice and step is the number of items to skip between items in the slice.

Basic Operators

There are several types of operators that can be used to perform various operations on variables and values.

Arithmetic Operators:

- +: addition
- -: subtraction
- *: multiplication
- /: division
- %: modulus (remainder)
- **: exponentiation
- //: floor division

Comparison Operators:

- ==: equal to
- !=: not equal to
- >: greater than
- <: less than
- >=: greater than or equal to
- <=: less than or equal to

Logical Operators:

- and: returns True if both operands are True
- or: returns True if one or both operands are True
- not: inverts the truth value of the operand

Assignment Operators:

- =: assigns a value to a variable
- +=: adds a value to a variable and assigns the result
- -=: subtracts a value from a variable and assigns the result
- *=: multiplies a variable by a value and assigns the result

- /=: divides a variable by a value and assigns the result
- %=: takes the modulus of a variable by a value and assigns the result
- **=: raises a variable to a power and assigns the result
- //=: performs floor division on a variable and assigns the result.

Identity Operators:

- is: returns True if both operands are the same object
- is not: returns True if both operands are not the same object

Membership Operators:

- in: returns True if the operand is in the sequence (e.g. list, tuple, string)
- not in: returns True if the operand is not in the sequence

Here's an example of using some of these operators:

```
x = 5
y = 2
print(x + y) # Output: 7
print(x - y) # Output: 3
print(x * y) # Output: 10
print(x / y) # Output: 2.5
print(x % y) # Output: 1
print(x ** y) # Output: 25
print(x // y) # Output: 2

x = True
y = False
print(x and y) # Output: False
print(x or y) # Output: True
print(not x) # Output: False
```

It is important to note that the order of operations (PEMDAS) is followed in Python, Parentheses, Exponents, Multiplication and Division, Addition and Subtraction.

String Formatting

String formatting is used to substitute placeholders in a string with values. The placeholders are represented by curly braces {}. There are several ways to format strings in Python, including the format() method, f-strings, and string concatenation.

The format() method is used to replace placeholders in a string with values. For example:

```
name = "John"
age = 30
print("My name is {} and I am {} years old.".format(name, age))
```

Output:

```
My name is John and I am 30 years old.
```

F-strings, also known as formatted string literals, were intro-
duced in Python 3.6 and provide a concise and convenient way
to embed expressions inside string literals.

For example:

```
name = "John"
age = 30
print(f"My name is {name} and I am {age} years old.")
```

Output:

```
My name is John and I am 30 years old.
```

String concatenation is another way to format strings in Python
by using the + operator to join multiple strings together.

For example:

```
name = "John"
age = 30
print("My name is " + name + " and I am " + str(age) + " years old.")
```

Output:

```
My name is John and I am 30 years old.
```

Basic String Operations

There are several basic string operations that you can perform, including concatenation, repetition, and indexing.

Concatenation is the process of joining two or more strings together. You can concatenate strings in Python using the + operator. For example:

```
string1 = "Hello"
string2 = "World"
string3 = string1 + " " + string2
print(string3)
```

Output: Hello World

Repetition is the process of repeating a string multiple times.

You can repeat a string in Python using the * operator. For example:

```
string = "Python "
print(string * 3)
```

Output: Python Python Python

Indexing is the process of accessing individual characters in a string by their position. In Python, strings are indexed starting from 0. For example:

```
string = "Python"
print(string[0])
```

Output: P

In addition to the above operations, you can also perform other operations like slicing, substring checking, string length, string method, etc.

```
string = "Python is a great language."
print(string[7:13]) # 'is a '
print('great' in string) #True
print(len(string)) # 27
print(string.upper()) #'PYTHON IS A GREAT LANGUAGE.'
```

Conditions

Conditions are used to control the flow of a program's execution. A condition is an expression that evaluates to either True or False.

The most basic form of a condition is a comparison between two values. For example:

```
x = 5
y = 10
if x < y:
    print("x is less than y")
```

Output: x is less than y

You can also use comparison operators like == (equal to), != (not equal to), > (greater than), < (less than), >= (greater than or equal to), and <= (less than or equal to) to create conditions. For example:

```
x = 5
y = 10
if x != y:
    print("x and y are not equal")
```

Output: x and y are not equal

You can also use logical operators like and, or, and not to combine multiple conditions. For example:

```
x = 5
y = 10
z = 15
if x < y and x < z:
    print("x is the smallest")
```

Output: x is the smallest

You can also use the keyword "in" to check whether a value is present in a sequence like a list, tuple, or string. For example:

```
list = [1, 2, 3, 4, 5]
if 4 in list:
    print("4 is present in the list")
```

Output: 4 is present in the list

In addition to the if statement, you can use the "if-else" or "if-elif-else" statement to handle multiple conditions.

```
x = 5
if x > 0:
    print("x is positive")
else:
    print("x is non-positive")
```

```
x = 5
if x > 0:
    print("x is positive")
elif x == 0:
    print("x is zero")
else:
    print("x is negative")
```

In this way, you can use conditions in Python to control the flow of your program and make it more dynamic and responsive to different inputs.

Loops

Loops are used to repeatedly execute a block of code. There are two types of loops in Python: for loops and while loops.

A for loop is used to iterate over a sequence of elements, such as a list, tuple, or string. The basic structure of a for loop is as follows:

```
numbers = [1, 2, 3, 4, 5]
for number in numbers:
    print(number)
```

Output:

```
1
2
3
4
5
```

A while loop is used to repeatedly execute a block of code as long as a certain condition is true. The basic structure of a while loop is as follows:

```
i = 1
while i <= 5:
    print(i)
    i = i + 1
```

Output:

```
1
2
3
4
5
```

You can also use the "break" and "continue" statements to control the flow of a loop. The "break" statement is used to exit a loop prematurely, while the "continue" statement is used to skip to the next iteration of a loop.

```
for number in range(1, 11):
    if number == 5:
        break
    print(number)
```

Output:

```
1
2
3
4
```

```
for number in range(1, 11):
    if number % 2 == 0:
        continue
    print(number)
```

Output:

```
1
3
5
7
9
```

With the help of loops, you can perform repetitive tasks efficiently and make your code more organized and readable.

Functions

A function is a block of organized, reusable code that performs a specific task. Functions are used to break down a larger program into smaller, more manageable pieces.

Creating a function in Python is done using the "def" keyword, followed by the function name, and a set of parentheses that can contain parameters. The code that makes up the function is indented under the function definition. For example:

```python
def greet(name):
    """This function greets the person passed in as a parameter"""
    print(f"Hello, {name}. Welcome!")

greet("John")
```

Output: Hello, John. Welcome!

Functions can also return a value using the "return" statement.

18

For example:

```
def add(x, y):
    """This function adds two numbers and return the result"""
    return x + y

result = add(5, 10)
print(result)
```

Output: 15

Functions can also have default values for the parameters, so if the user does not provide any value for that parameter, the default value is used.

```
def power(x, y=2):
    """This function raises x to the power of y"""
    return x ** y

print(power(5)) #25
print(power(5,3)) #125
```

Functions can also take an arbitrary number of arguments using the *args and **kwargs. "*args" is used to pass a non-keyworded variable-length argument list, and "**kwargs" is used to pass a keyworded variable-length argument list.

```python
def test_function(*args, **kwargs):
    for arg in args:
        print(arg)
    for key, value in kwargs.items():
        print(f"{key} = {value}")

test_function(1, 2, 3, name="John", age=25)
```

Output:

```
1
2
3
name = John
age = 25
```

Functions can also be defined inside another function and can also be passed as an argument to another function, which are called nested functions and functions as objects, respectively.

Functions are a powerful tool in Python and help you write more organized and reusable code. They are particularly useful for breaking down a large program into smaller, more manageable pieces, which makes the code easier to understand, maintain, and test.

Classes and Objects

Class is a blueprint for creating objects (a particular data structure), providing initial values for states (member variables or attributes), and implementing behaviors (member functions or methods).

Creating a class is done using the "class" keyword, followed by the class name. For example:

```
class Person:
    def __init__(self, name, age):
        self.name = name
        self.age = age

p1 = Person("John", 30)
print(p1.name)
print(p1.age)
```

Output: John
   30

The "init" method is a special method that is called when an object of the class is created, and it is used to initialize the object's attributes. "self" is a reference to the object being created, and it is used to access the object's attributes and methods.

In the class, you can define class variables and class methods, which are shared by all objects of the class. Class variables are defined outside of any method; usually, they are placed at the top, right after the class header, and class methods are defined using the @classmethod decorator. For example:

```
class Person:
    count = 0
    def __init__(self, name, age):
        self.name = name
        self.age = age
        Person.count += 1

    @classmethod
    def display_count(cls):
        print(f"Total Person: {cls.count}")

p1 = Person("John", 30)
p2 = Person("Mary", 25)
p3 = Person("Bob", 35)

Person.display_count()
```

Output: Total Person:3

Objects in Python can also be created from classes and are known as instances of a class. Each object has its own distinct state and behavior, but they are created from the same class, which defines a common set of properties and methods.

Classes and objects are fundamental concepts in object-oriented programming and allow you to model real-world concepts and entities in your code, making it more organized, reusable, and maintainable.

Dictionaries

A dictionary is a collection of key-value pairs, where each key is unique and is used to access the associated value. Dictionaries are also known as associative arrays, maps, or hash maps.

You can create a dictionary using curly braces {} and separate the keys and values using a colon: For example:

```
person = {"name": "John", "age": 30}
print(person["name"])
print(person["age"])
```

Output:

```
John
30
```

You can also use the dict() constructor to create a dictionary. For example:

```
person = dict(name="John", age=30)
print(person["name"])
print(person["age"])
```

You can add new key-value pairs to a dictionary by assigning a value to a new key, or you can modify the value of an existing key by reassigning its value. For example:

```
person = {"name": "John", "age": 30}
person["gender"] = "male"
print(person)
person["age"] = 35
print(person)
```

Output:

```
{'name': 'John', 'age': 30, 'gender': 'male'}
{'name': 'John', 'age': 35, 'gender': 'male'}
```

You can remove key-value pairs from a dictionary using the "del" keyword or the "pop()" method. The "del" keyword removes the key-value pair with the specified key, and the "pop()" method removes the key-value pair with the specified key and returns its value.

```
person = {"name": "John", "age": 30, "gender":"male"}
del person["gender"]
print(person)
gender = person.pop("gender", "not found")
print(gender)
```

Dictionaries have useful built-in methods like "keys()", "values()" and "items()" which returns the keys, values and key-value pairs respectively.

```
person = {"name": "John", "age": 30}
print(person.keys())
print(person.values())
print(person.items())
```

Output:

```
dict_keys(['name', 'age'])
dict_values(['John', 30])
dict_items([('name', 'John'), ('age', 30)])
```

Dictionaries are widely used in Python for many tasks, such as counting occurrences of items in a list, storing configuration settings or settings for an application, and many more. They provide a fast and efficient way to access and store data, making them a powerful tool for any Python programmer.

Modules and Packages

The module is a single file that contains Python definitions and statements. Modules allow you to organize your code into reusable and maintainable chunks. You can create your own modules by creating a file with a .py extension and writing functions, classes, and other definitions inside it.

You can use a module in another script by using the "import" statement. For example, if you have a module called "mymodule.py" that contains a function called "greet()", you can use it in another script like this:

```
import mymodule
mymodule.greet("John")
```

You can also use the "from" keyword to import specific objects from a module, like this:

```
from mymodule import greet
greet("John")
```

A package is a collection of modules that are organized in a directory hierarchy. Packages provide a way to organize related modules and provide a namespace for the modules. The package name is used as a prefix for the modules inside the package.

To create a package, you need to create a directory with the package name, and then place the modules inside the directory. The package directory should also contain a file named init.py which can be empty or can contain initialization code for the package.

You can use a module inside a package by importing it with the package name as a prefix. For example, if you have a package named "mypackage" that contains a module named "mymodule", you can use it like this:

```
import mypackage.mymodule
mypackage.mymodule.greet("John")
```

You can also use the "from" keyword to import specific objects from a module, like this:

```
from mypackage.mymodule import greet
greet("John")
```

Modules and packages are powerful tools that allow you to organize and reuse your code in a structured way, making it easier to understand, maintain, and share with others. Python has a lot of built-in modules and packages and you can also install 3rd party modules and packages using package manager like pip.

Advanced Concepts

Generators

Generator is a special kind of function that allows you to iterate over a sequence of items, without the need to create the entire sequence in memory. A generator function is defined like a normal function, but instead of using the "return" statement, it uses the "yield" statement to return a value.

When a generator function is called, it returns a generator object, which is an iterator that can be used to iterate over the items produced by the generator function. Each time the generator's "next()" method is called, the function's code is executed from the last point of execution, until it encounters the "yield" statement, which returns the value and suspends the execution of the function.

For example, you can use a generator function to generate the Fibonacci sequence:

```
def fibonacci(n):
    a, b = 0, 1
    for i in range(n):
        yield a
        a, b = b, a + b

for number in fibonacci(10):
    print(number)
```

Output:

```
0
1
1
2
3
5
8
13
21
34
```

Using a generator function has some advantages over using a normal function:

- Memory Efficiency: Generators don't store all the values in memory like a list, it only stores the current state of the generator function.
- Fast: Generators are faster than normal functions because they don't need to return all the values at once, they return one value at a time.
- Easy to Implement: Generators are easy to implement and are a good alternative to complex data structures like lists,

tuples, and dictionaries.
- Easy to Debug: Generators are easy to debug and test because they only execute one line at a time

Generators are widely used in Python for a variety of tasks, such as reading large files, generating sequences of data, and implementing iteration patterns in object-oriented programming.

List Comprehensions

List comprehensions are a concise and efficient way to create lists in Python. They allow you to create a new list by applying an operation to each item in an existing list (or other iterable), and optionally filtering the items based on some condition.

The basic syntax of a list comprehension is as follows:

```
new_list = [expression for item in iterable if condition]
```

For example, you can use list comprehension to create a new list of squares of the numbers from 1 to 10:

```
squares = [x**2 for x in range(1, 11)]
print(squares)
```

Output: [1, 4, 9, 16, 25, 36, 49, 64, 81, 100]

You can also use a list comprehension to filter the items based on some conditions:

```
even_squares = [x**2 for x in range(1, 11) if x % 2 == 0]
print(even_squares)
```

Output: [4, 16, 36, 64, 100]

You can also use list comprehension to create a new list by applying a function to each item:

```
words = ['cat', 'dog', 'elephant']
lengths = [len(word) for word in words]
print(lengths)
```

Output: [3, 3, 8]

List comprehensions are more concise and readable than equivalent for loops and are useful for simple cases where you need to create a new list from an existing one. They can also be more efficient than loops, especially when creating large lists, as they avoid the creation of a new list object for each iteration.

List comprehension with multiple conditions and nested loops, while still readable, can be harder to understand and less efficient than using separate loops and if statements.

Lambda functions

Lambda function is a small, anonymous function that is defined using the "lambda" keyword. It is used to create small, throw-away functions for one-time use. They are also known as lambda expressions and are similar to closures in other programming languages.

The basic syntax of a lambda function is as follows:

```
lambda arguments: expression
```

For example, you can use a lambda function to square a number:

```
square = lambda x: x**2
print(square(5))
```

Output: 25

You can also use lambda functions in combination with built-in functions such as filter(), map(), and reduce() to apply a function to a sequence of items. For example, you can use the filter() function to filter a list of numbers based on a lambda function:

```
numbers = [1, 2, 3, 4, 5, 6, 7, 8, 9, 10]
even_numbers = list(filter(lambda x: x % 2 == 0, numbers))
print(even_numbers)
```

Output: [2, 4, 6, 8, 10]

You can also use the map() function to apply a lambda function to a sequence of items:

```
squared_numbers = list(map(lambda x: x**2, numbers))
print(squared_numbers)
```

Output: [1, 4, 9, 16, 25, 36, 49, 64, 81, 100]

Lambda functions are useful for creating small, throwaway functions for one-time use and for passing functions as arguments to higher-order functions such as filter() and map(). They are also useful in situations where a function is needed as a short-lived and throwaway object.

It is important to keep in mind that lambda functions are limited in functionality and are not recommended for complex tasks. They are best used for simple operations that can be defined in one line of code.

*args and **kwargs

*args and **kwargs syntax is used to define functions that can accept a variable number of arguments.

The *args syntax allows you to pass a variable number of positional arguments to a function. It is used to pass a tuple of arguments to a function. For example:

```python
def print_args(*args):
    for arg in args:
        print(arg)

print_args(1, 2, 3, 4, 5)
```

Output:

```
1
2
3
4
5
```

The **kwargs syntax allows you to pass a variable number of keyword arguments to a function. It is used to pass a dictionary of arguments to a function. For example:

```python
def print_kwargs(**kwargs):
    for key, value in kwargs.items():
        print(key, value)

print_kwargs(name="John", age=30)
```

Output:

```
name John
age 30
```

You can also use the *args and **kwargs syntax together in a function definition, to accept a variable number of both positional and keyword arguments. For example:

```python
def print_args_kwargs(*args, **kwargs):
    for arg in args:
        print(arg)
    for key, value in kwargs.items():
        print(key, value)

print_args_kwargs(1, 2, 3, name="John", age=30)
```

Output:

```
1
2
3
name John
age 30
```

The *args and **kwargs syntax is useful in many situations, such as when a function needs to accept a variable number of arguments, or when a function needs to accept a variable number of arguments of different types. It also allows a function to be more flexible and reusable.

Regular Expressions

Regular expressions are patterns used to match strings or parts of strings. The module re provides full support for Perl-like regular expressions in Python.

A regular expression is a sequence of characters that defines a search pattern. The search pattern can be used to match (and sometimes replace) strings, or to perform some other manipulation of strings.

Here are some examples of regular expressions and their usage in Python:

```
import re

# Find all occurrences of the word "cat" in a string
text = "The cat in the hat."
x = re.findall("cat", text)
print(x)
```

Output: ['cat']

```
# Search for a digit in a string
text = "There are 2 types of people."
x = re.search("\d", text)
print(x.group())
```

Output: 2

```
# Replace all occurrences of the word "dog" with the word "cat" in a
string
text = "The dog is a domesticated mammal."
x = re.sub("dog", "cat", text)
print(x)
```

Output: The cat is a domesticated mammal.

```
# Find all occurrences of words starting with "s" and ending with "t"
text = "It is a small world."
x = re.findall("s\w+t", text)
print(x)
```

Output: ['small']

The re module provides many other useful functions like split(), compile(), etc.

Regular expressions are a powerful tool for working with text and are widely used in many areas such as data validation, text parsing, and data cleaning.

It is important to note that regular expressions can be tricky to master and it is often easier to use regular expression libraries or tools to build and test your regular expressions before using them in your code.

Exception Handling

Exception handling is a mechanism to handle errors or exceptions that occur during the execution of a program. When an error occurs, an exception is raised, and the normal flow of the program is interrupted. To handle exceptions, you can use try-except statements to catch and handle the exception.

The basic syntax of try-except statement is as follows:

```
try:
    # code that may raise an exception
except ExceptionType:
    # code that will be executed if the exception is raised
```

For example, you can use a try-except statement to handle a ZeroDivisionError exception:

```
try:
    x = 1 / 0
except ZeroDivisionError:
    print("Cannot divide by zero")
```

Output: Cannot divide by zero

You can also use the else clause to specify code that will be executed if no exception is raised:

Output: 0.5

You can also use the finally clause to specify code that will be executed regardless of whether an exception is raised or not: Output: Cannot divide by zero

This will be executed no matter what

You can also catch multiple exception types by specifying multiple except clauses:

39

```
try:
    x = int("hello")
except ValueError:
    print("Cannot convert to integer")
except TypeError:
    print("Cannot convert to int")
```

Output: Cannot convert to integer

It is important to handle exceptions properly in your code to
ensure that your program can continue to run even if errors
occur and to provide useful error messages to the user. It is also
a good practice to raise your own exceptions when necessary,
to indicate that a specific error has occurred, and to provide
additional information about the error.

Sets

Set is an unordered collection of unique items. Sets are defined
using curly braces {} or the built-in set() function.

Here are some examples of how to create and use sets in Python:

```
# create a set
fruits = {"apple", "banana", "orange"}
print(fruits)
```

```python
# create an empty set
fruits = set()

# add items to the set
fruits.add("apple")
fruits.add("banana")
fruits.add("orange")
print(fruits)
```

```python
# check if an item is in a set
fruits = {"apple", "banana", "orange"}
if "banana" in fruits:
    print("banana is in the set")
```

```python
# remove an item from a set
fruits = {"apple", "banana", "orange"}
fruits.remove("banana")
print(fruits)
```

```
# set operations
fruits1 = {"apple", "banana", "orange"}
fruits2 = {"banana", "orange", "mango"}

# union
print(fruits1 | fruits2)
# or
print(fruits1.union(fruits2))

# intersection
print(fruits1 & fruits2)
# or
print(fruits1.intersection(fruits2))

# difference
print(fruits1 - fruits2)
# or
print(fruits1.difference(fruits2))
```

Output:

```
{'banana', 'orange', 'mango', 'apple'}
{'banana', 'orange', 'mango', 'apple'}
{'banana', 'orange'}
{'banana', 'orange'}
{'apple'}
{'apple'}
```

Sets are useful for tasks such as removing duplicates from a list, testing membership, and performing mathematical operations such as unions, intersections, and differences. They are also efficient for searching since searching for an item in a set is an O(1) operation on average.

Serialization

Serialization is the process of converting an object to a byte stream and deserialization is the process of recreating the object from the byte stream. This allows the object to be stored in a file, sent over the network, or even stored in a database.

Python provides several modules to perform serialization and deserialization, such as *pickle*, *JSON*, and *marshal*.

pickle is a built-in module in Python that can be used to serialize and deserialize Python objects. Here is an example of how to use a pickle to serialize an object:

```python
import pickle

# create an object
class Person:
    def __init__(self, name, age):
        self.name = name
        self.age = age

person = Person("John", 30)

# serialize the object
with open("person.pickle", "wb") as f:
    pickle.dump(person, f)
```

Here is an example of how to deserialize the object:

```python
import pickle

# deserialize the object
with open("person.pickle", "rb") as f:
    person = pickle.load(f)

print(person.name)
print(person.age)
```

Output: John, 30

JSON is another built-in module in Python that can be used to serialize and deserialize JSON (JavaScript Object Notation) data. Here is an example of how to use JSON to serialize an object:

```python
import json

# create an object
person = {"name": "John", "age": 30}

# serialize the object
with open("person.json", "w") as f:
    json.dump(person, f)
```

Partial functions

A partial function is a function that is created by "fixing" one or more arguments of an existing function. The functools module provides a partial() function which can be used to create a new function with some of the arguments already set. The new function, when called, will automatically pass the fixed arguments along with any new arguments.

Here's an example of how to use functools.partial() to create a new function that multiplies a number by a fixed factor:

```python
from functools import partial

def multiply(a, b):
    return a * b

# create a new function that multiplies by 2
double = partial(multiply, 2)

print(double(5)) # 10
```

In this example, the partial(multiply, 2) creates a new function double that is equivalent to multiply(2, b). When double(5) is called, it is equivalent to calling multiply(2, 5).

You can also pass keyword arguments when creating a partial function:

```python
from functools import partial

def greet(greeting, name):
    return f'{greeting}, {name}'

hi_john = partial(greet, name='John', greeting='Hi')
print(hi_john()) # Hi, John
```

functools.partial is useful when you have a function that takes multiple arguments, and you want to create a new function with some of the arguments fixed. This is especially useful when you need to pass a function as an argument to another function, and you want to fix some of the arguments so that they don't need to be passed every time.

Code Introspection

Code introspection is the ability to inspect and retrieve information about the code and the objects that it defines.

Python provides several built-in functions and modules that allow you to inspect the code and the objects at runtime.

Here are some examples of how to use code introspection in Python:

- dir() function returns a list of all attributes and methods of an object.

```
x = [1, 2, 3]
print(dir(x))
```

Output:

```
['__add__', '__class__', '__contains__', '__delattr__', '__delitem__',
'__dir__', '__doc__', '__eq__', '__format__', '__ge__',
'__getattribute__', '__getitem__', '__gt__', '__hash__', '__iadd__',
'__imul__', '__init__', '__init_subclass__', '__iter__', '__le__',
'__len__', '__lt__', '__mul__', '__ne__', '__new__', '__reduce__',
'__reduce_ex__', '__repr__', '__reversed__', '__rmul__', '__setattr__',
'__setitem__', '__sizeof__', '__str__', '__subclasshook__', 'append',
'clear', 'copy', 'count', 'extend', 'index', 'insert', 'pop', 'remove',
'reverse', 'sort']
```

- type() function returns the type of an object.

```
<class 'list'>
```

- id() function: This function returns the identity of an object. For example:

```
>>> a = 5
>>> b = 5
>>> id(a)
4435204064
>>> id(b)
4435204064
```

- inspect module: This module provides a number of useful functions for inspecting live objects, such as inspect.get-

47

members(), inspect.isclass(), and inspect.getdoc().

- doc attribute: This attribute returns the documentation string of an object, if it exists. For example:

```
>>> def foo():
    """This is the documentation string of the function."""
>>> print(foo.__doc__)
This is the documentation string of the function.
```

- name , module and class attributes: These attributes returns the name, module and class of an object respectively.
- hasattr(): This function returns True if the object has an attribute with the given name, and False otherwise.
- getattr(): This function returns the value of the attribute with the given name. If the attribute doesn't exist, it raises an AttributeError exception.
- setattr(): This function sets the value of the attribute with the given name. If the attribute doesn't exist, it creates a new attribute with the given name and value.
- delattr(): This function deletes the attribute with the given name. If the attribute doesn't exist, it raises an attributeError exception.

Closures

Closure is a nested function that remembers the values in the enclosing scope even if they are not present in memory. Closures have access to variables in the enclosing scope, even after the outer function has finished executing.

Here's an example of a closure in Python:

```
def outer_function(x):
    def inner_function(y):
        return x + y
    return inner_function

closure = outer_function(10)
print(closure(5)) # 15
```

In this example, the outer_function takes an argument x and returns the inner_function. The inner_function takes an argument y and returns the sum of x and y. The inner_function is a closure because it remembers the value of x even after the outer_function has finished executing.

Closures can also be used to create decorators, which are functions that modify the behavior of other functions. Here's an example of a simple decorator that adds a prefix to the string returned by a function:

```python
def prefix_decorator(prefix):
    def decorator(func):
        def wrapper(*args, **kwargs):
            return prefix + func(*args, **kwargs)
        return wrapper
    return decorator

@prefix_decorator("Mr. ")
def get_name():
    return "John Smith"

print(get_name()) # "Mr. John Smith"
```

In this example, prefix_decorator is a closure that takes a prefix argument and returns a decorator function that takes a func argument and returns a wrapper function. The wrapper function calls the original func with the same arguments and prefixes the result with the value of '

Decorators

Decorators are functions that modify the behavior of other functions. Decorators are a powerful and elegant way to add functionality to existing functions, without modifying the original code.

A decorator is a function that takes another function as an argument and returns a new function that usually extends the behavior of the original function.

Here's an example of a simple decorator that adds a prefix to

50

the string returned by a function:

```
def prefix_decorator(func):
    def wrapper(*args, **kwargs):
        return "Mr. " + func(*args, **kwargs)
    return wrapper

@prefix_decorator
def get_name():
    return "John Smith"

print(get_name()) # "Mr. John Smith"
```

In this example, prefix_decorator is a decorator that takes a func argument and returns a wrapper function. The wrapper function calls the original func with the same arguments and prefixes the result with the string "Mr. ". The @prefix_decorator notation is a shorthand for get_name = prefix_decorator(get_name)

You can also use decorators with arguments by using inner functions, like this:

51

```
def prefix_decorator(prefix):
    def decorator(func):
        def wrapper(*args, **kwargs):
            return prefix + func(*args, **kwargs)
        return wrapper
    return decorator

@prefix_decorator("Mr.")
def get_name():
    return "John Smith"

print(get_name()) # "Mr. John Smith"
```

Decorators are widely used in Python web frameworks like Flask and Django, to add functionality such as authentication,

logging, and caching to views and route handlers. They are also commonly used to add decorators to functions to measure execution time, and perform input and validation.

Map, Filter, Reduce

map, **filter**, and **reduce** are built-in Python functions that allow for functional programming.

map applies a given function to all elements of an input list and returns an iterator to the resulting list. For example:

```
numbers = [1, 2, 3, 4]
squared_numbers = map(lambda x: x**2, numbers)
# squared_numbers is now an iterator containing [1, 4, 9, 16]
```

filter filters elements from an input list based on a given function and returns an iterator to the resulting list. For example:

```
numbers = [1, 2, 3, 4, 5, 6]
even_numbers = filter(lambda x: x % 2 == 0, numbers)
# even_numbers is now an iterator containing [2, 4, 6].
```

reduce applies a given function cumulatively to the elements of an input list, from left to right, so as to reduce the list to a single value. For example:

```
from functools import reduce
numbers = [1, 2, 3, 4, 5]
product = reduce(lambda x, y: x*y, numbers)
# product is now 120 (1*2*3*4*5)
```

Note that in python3 map, filter, and reduce returns map object, and filter object respectively, to get the actual list out of them we need to pass them to **list**() function.

Data Science Libraries

Numpy Arrays

Numpy is a powerful library for Python that provides support for large, multi-dimensional arrays and matrices of numerical data, as well as a large collection of high-level mathematical functions to operate on these arrays.

A Numpy array is a grid of values, all of the same type, and is indexed by a tuple of nonnegative integers. The number of dimensions is the rank of the array; the shape of an array is a tuple of integers giving the size of the array along each dimension.

You can create a Numpy array by using the numpy.array() function. For example:

```
import numpy as np
a = np.array([1, 2, 3])
print(a)
```

Output: [1 2 3]

You can also create arrays with multiple dimensions by passing a list of lists to the numpy.array() function. For example:

```
b = np.array([[1, 2, 3], [4, 5, 6]])
print(b)
```

Output:

```
[[1 2 3]
 [4 5 6]]
```

You can also create arrays with a specific shape and type using the numpy.zeros(), numpy.ones(), and numpy.empty() functions.

```
c = np.zeros((3,4))
print(c)
```

Output:

```
[[0. 0. 0. 0.]
 [0. 0. 0. 0.]
 [0. 0. 0. 0.]]
```

```
d = np.ones((2,3), dtype=np.int)
print(d)
```

Output:

```
[[1 1 1]
 [1 1 1]]
```

Numpy arrays are more efficient than Python lists for numerical operations because they allow you to perform element-wise operations (such as addition, subtraction, multiplication, etc.) on entire arrays, and they also provide more advanced mathematical functions such as linear algebra, Fourier transform, and more.

Numpy arrays are widely used in scientific computing, data analysis, machine learning, and many other fields for their ease of use and efficiency.

Pandas Basics

Pandas is a powerful library for Python that provides easy-to-use data structures and data analysis tools for handling and manipulating numerical tables and time series data. It is built on top of the Numpy library and is an essential tool for data science and machine learning tasks.

The two primary data structures in Pandas are Series and DataFrame. A Series is a one-dimensional array-like object that can hold any data type and is similar to a column in a spreadsheet or a dataset. A DataFrame is a two-dimensional table of data with rows and columns, similar to a spreadsheet or a SQL table.

You can create a Series by passing a list or array of data to the pandas.Series() function and specifying an index. For example:

```
import pandas as pd
s = pd.Series([1, 3, 5, np.nan, 6, 8])
print(s)
```

Output:

```
0    1.0
1    3.0
2    5.0
3    NaN
4    6.0
5    8.0
dtype: float64
```

You can create a DataFrame by passing a NumPy array, a Python list of lists, a Python dictionary, or a pandas Series to the pandas.DataFrame() function. For example:

57

```
import numpy as np

data = {'name': ['John', 'Mary', 'Bob'],
        'age': [30, 25, 35],
        'gender': ['male
```

Afterword

As you reach the end of "Python for Beginners: A Step-by-Step Introduction to Programming with Python," you've not only completed a book but began a transforming journey into the world of programming. Acquiring proficiency in a new language, be it spoken or computer-based, necessitates persistence, patience, and practice. The knowledge and abilities you have gained from this book serve as the foundation for a much bigger structure.

Recall that the information you have learned here is only the beginning. The field of programming is quite broad and always changing. Your current knowledge provides a strong base on which to build increasingly intricate projects, investigate specific fields, or even experiment with different programming languages.

The most valuable takeaway from this experience is not only about Python; rather, it's about the ability to solve problems, think logically, and experience the simple joy of creativity that comes with programming. Accept the challenges that lie ahead since they will give you the chance to develop and learn new things.

Finally, this is not where the voyage ends. Continue exploring, building, and coding. Collaborate with others, impart your knowledge, and never lose your curiosity. Programming is a universe that is ready for your input.

Well done for finishing this book. You've made the first, most important step in learning how to program in Python. There are a ton of fascinating and limitless opportunities ahead of us. Take pleasure in the trip and let your enthusiasm for coding lead the way.

Happy coding!

About the Author

Serhan Sarı is a software engineer and accomplished author with a passion for both technology and the written word. His diverse range of interests includes martial arts, snowboarding, and the intricate world of coding.

As a software engineer, Serhan has demonstrated an exceptional aptitude for crafting innovative solutions and developing software applications that make a meaningful impact. His commitment to the field of technology has led him to create and contribute to various projects, showcasing his dedication to the ever-evolving world of software development.

In addition to his technical prowess, Serhan is a published author, where he channels his creativity and storytelling abilities. Through his written works, he takes readers on captivating journeys, revealing intricate plots and thought-provoking narratives.

Outside of the digital realm, Serhan finds solace and excitement in the realm of martial arts. He continuously hones his skills, mastering various disciplines that require discipline, physical prowess, and mental acuity. Whether it's on the mat or in the dojo, he exemplifies dedication and commitment.

When winter graces the land with its snowy touch, you'll often find Serhan on the slopes, snowboarding with a sense of adventure. He embraces the thrill of carving through fresh powder, demonstrating a fearless spirit and a zest for life's exhilarating moments.

Serhan Sarı's life is a blend of technological innovation, literary creativity, martial arts discipline, and the adrenaline of snowboarding. With an insatiable curiosity and a determined spirit, he continues to explore new horizons, always eager to take on the next challenge.

You can connect with me on:
🌐 https://www.serhansari.com

Also by Serhan Sari

Python Toolbox: 100 Scripts for Developers

"Python Toolbox: 100 Scripts for Developers" is a comprehensive collection designed to empower programmers with a treasure trove of ready-to-use Python scripts. From automating tasks to building robust applications, this book serves as a practical guide, offering 100 meticulously crafted scripts, complete with explanations and implementation tips. Whether you're a seasoned developer or just stepping into the world of Python, this toolbox provides a versatile resource, unlocking the potential of Python for diverse programming needs.

Unexpected Departures: Real Stories of Tragic Endings

"Unexpected Departures: Real Stories of Tragic Endings" is a compelling book that delves deep into the lives of ordinary individuals who found themselves in extraordinary and heart-wrenching situations. The stories within this collection are drawn from real-life experiences and narrated with raw emotion, offering a powerful glimpse into the human condition when faced with sudden, tragic events.

The book covers a wide spectrum of tragic endings, from personal losses to life-altering accidents and even unforeseen twists of fate. The common thread running through these narratives is the resilience and courage displayed by the people who lived through these trying moments. Their stories serve as a testament to the indomitable spirit of humanity.

With a focus on personal narratives, "Unexpected Departures" invites readers to connect with the deeply human side of tragedy. It explores the emotional journeys that follow such unexpected endings, including the grief, hope, and healing that come with them. These stories not only provide insights into the fragility of life but also offer a profound exploration of the strength of the human spirit in the face of adversity.

Readers of "Unexpected Departures" will be moved and inspired by real-life accounts, finding solace and empathy in the shared experiences of those who have navigated their way through unforeseen tragedies. This book is a touching reminder of our common humanity and the power of resilience when life takes unexpected turns.

www.ingramcontent.com/pod-product-compliance
Lightning Source LLC
LaVergne TN
LVHW051740050326
832903LV00023B/1030